The
Children's Ketubah Project

by Heidi Cooper

foreword by Anne Elliott

Foreword

I first arrived on Heidi Cooper's website a few years ago, when I found her homeschooling ideas based upon the Torah portions. My husband had just left the ministry, as a Baptist pastor, and our family was learning how to live out the Torah in our home every day. I purchased her *My First Torah* book to read with my young children, because I had no idea how to start teaching Torah to my children when I didn't even know it very well myself.

I have been impressed not only with Heidi's creativity and ability to make Torah living practical, but I'm incredibly thankful that she sticks to Scripture. The Torah seems to be written on the walls and gates of her home, but most of all on her heart – which is why she's so gifted at impressing it upon her children.

I'm pretty tough on the parenting books I read. I don't want a bunch of psychology. I want Scripture, with plenty of instruction for how to apply it to my family, especially after I've messed up and need to correct the consequences of sinful choices we've all made in the past. Not very many parenting books make it to my "like" list.

Heidi's book is at the very top of my list! Scripture is her very foundation, especially the wisdom of Torah, which was written for parents to teach to their children, after all. She also tackles tough issues like discipline, and I don't feel like she was too afraid to talk about it! Best of all, since I have seven children of my own, I know that her gentle but biblical advice actually works.

I am now a homeschool curriculum author, and as such, I talk with Torah-keeping families on a daily basis. I am convinced that the biggest issue facing our families is parenting. YHVH desires a godly seed from our marriages, but this is exactly why the Enemy fights so hard against us.

As you read the pages of this book and consider making a covenant to your children, to teach them in the peaceable ways of Torah and to dedicate them to the service of the King of Kings, ask Him to give you wisdom on how to apply it to your home this week. Find other families who will also answer the call. Together, we will raise up an army of children for YHVH!

~ Anne Elliott

www.homeschoolingtorah.com
www.anneelliott.com
www.foundationspress.com

Introduction

This is a book about parenting. I hope it will be more than just another how-to book, but will rather encourage you to rise to the great challenge of raising your children and leaving a positive mark on the next generation. This is a book about commitment, commitment to your spouse and commitment to your children. It's also a book about YHVH's commitment to us. I pray it is a blessing to you.

This book was first self-published in 2010. I have updated and expanded the material since then. Each section now has a notes section and I encourage you to write all over it. This book makes a great foundation for a group study about parenting as well. Enjoy!

Why talk about ketubahs in a parenting book? A ketubah is a written marriage contract between a husband and a wife. They enter into a covenant relationship and the ketubah lays out the terms. Traditionally, a ketubah is written and decorated beautifully and hung on the couple's wall. Each day, they can look at it and remember their commitment to their spouse and the responsibilities they have. YHVH (the personal name of the God of Abraham, Isaac, and Jacob) made a covenant with His people, the Children of Israel. The Torah, the first five books of the Bible, tells the story of how He built the nation of Israel, brought them out of Egypt, and made a covenant with them. The Ten Commandments that He gave them on Mount Sinai could be considered His ketubah, His written contract with us, His bride.

What if we wrote a ketubah for our children? What if we wrote down our responsibilities as a parent and our commitment to our children? What if we showed it to our children to help them understand our love and commitment? How would our children respond? How would it change them? How would it change us?

The Children's Ketubah Project is a challenge to parents. We wanted to know what would happen in families if we wrote ketubahs for our children. Many families have already done so, and it helped them to grow closer together as a family, and raise their children with purpose. Will you join them? In this book, you will find a suggested ketubah, along with Scriptural support for its content. We will also cover the importance of the weekly blessing. The last chapter contains additional resources that you may find helpful as a parent. Please join us as we seek to bless the next generation.

To keep things clear, a covenant is a promise made between two parties. A contract is essentially the same as a covenant. A ketubah is the written form of either a covenant or contract, traditionally used for weddings, but sometimes for other events. Throughout the book, you will see me use the Hebrew name for our God, YHVH, and Yeshua for our Messiah.

Hear, O Israel: The LORD our God is one LORD.

And thou shalt love the LORD thy God with all thine heart, and with all thy soul, and with all thy might.

And these words, which I command thee this day, shall be in thine heart:

And thou shalt teach them diligently unto thy children, and shalt talk of them when thou sittest in thine house, and when thou walkest by the way, and when thou liest down, and when thou risest up.

And thou shalt bind them for a sign upon thine hand, and they shall be as frontlets between thine eyes.

And thou shalt write them upon the posts of thy house, and on thy gates.

Deuteronomy 6:4-9

Table of Contents

Chapter 1

The Idea

And God said, "This is the token of the covenant which I make between me and you and every living creature that is with you, for perpetual generations: I do set my bow in the cloud, and it shall be for a token of a covenant between me and the earth."

Genesis 9:12-13

I sometimes struggle with the daily aspects of parenting. It is easy to forget my priorities as I tend to meals, bedtime, and schoolwork. At the end of the day, I didn't read a story to them. I spoke rather harshly. I sent them outside so I could have time to myself. I was left with another day survived, but nothing really gained. How could I break out of the cycle? How could I remember to accomplish what was really important and value each day as a parent?

One day, I was studying the life of Noah, and the beautiful covenant that YHVH made with Noah. He promised that He would never flood the whole earth again. A rainbow was put in the sky as an everlasting covenant between Him and all mankind.

I immediately thought of Abraham and the covenant made with him. Abraham cut the animals in two (except the birds) and YHVH walked through the pieces as Abraham slept. I always found it curious that Abraham never walked through the pieces. Usually all parties in a covenant will "sign the papers" or agree to the terms. When my husband and I got married, we both made a vow and signed a marriage contract. We were equally responsible to hold up our end of the deal. However, when YHVH made a covenant with Abraham, Abraham did not "sign."

I think part of the reasoning might be that YHVH chose Abraham to be His "child." He knew that Abraham and his descendants would not be able to fulfill their responsibilities, so He made a covenant in which only He was responsible to uphold the terms. What a blessing that is!

> *He made a covenant in which only He was responsible to uphold the terms.*

It occurred to me that we could do the same for our children. We could make a commitment to be faithful parents to them, but we would be the only one signing. We couldn't make excuses for our failures like, "He's a difficult child." We would be accepting all responsibility for the upbringing of the children YHVH has blessed us with. When we commit ourselves to the task in writing, we will most likely rise to the challenge. We can't do a perfect job in this human, flawed body, but we can be faithful. We can be purposeful. With YHVH's help, we can be successful.

I called my Mom and asked why we don't have ketubahs for our children. She knew about ketubahs at weddings, but had never heard of anything in regards to children. I began to wonder why.

Reason #1 We are afraid that we cannot do it right.

Perhaps we are scared that we won't be able to hold up our end of the bargain if we make a covenant with our children. That is a completely legitimate fear. Let me ease your fear right now. You can't do a perfect job, and that is okay. Did you catch that? You and I are not perfect parents. It grieves me to think of some of the mistakes I have made, the angry words, the brush-offs, the failure to train properly. If I wrote down my responsibilities as a parent and promised my child that I would fulfill my responsibilities, I would be a liar. But YHVH gave me children and told me to raise them right. There must be a way.

I think that the answer might be in Philippians 4:13.

I can do all things through Christ which strengtheneth me.

Philippians 4:13

At the very moment that we admit we are not fit for the job, our help arrives. YHVH is quick to help those who are humble and teachable. He is ready to give us everything we need to prepare our children for life. But if we act like we have all the answers, He is not going to offer His help. We have made it clear that we don't need His assistance.

The benefit of writing down our responsibilities is to keep us focused and accountable and to demonstrate to our children that we are serious and committed to their well-being. We want to see them succeed and prosper. More importantly, however, we want to give them a spiritual inheritance. We want them to be confident in their relationship with YHVH, able to stand strong even without Mom and Dad. We won't be perfect, but we can be successful.

Reason #2 We don't know what our responsibilities are.

If we don't know, or are uncertain what we are supposed to be doing, then we have no time to waste. Children do come with an instruction manual. It's called Torah, and all the Scripture written after Torah. But sometimes we have to dig a little to get the answers we seek.

Scripture is full of guidance for parents. YHVH is our Heavenly Father. We are His children. We should deal with our children the same way He deals with us. Look at how He treats His children. Ask Him for wisdom. He will guide you with the truth of His word. Here are some verses to get you started on your quest for truth.

Train up a child in the way he should go: and when he is old, he will not depart from it.

Proverbs 22:6

My son, attend to my words; incline thine ear unto my sayings. Let them not depart from thine eyes; keep them in the midst of thine heart. For they are life unto those that find them, and health to all their flesh.

Proverbs 4:20-22

In the fear of the LORD is strong confidence: and his children shall have a place of refuge.

Proverbs 14:26

Therefore all things whatsoever ye would that men should do to you, do ye even so to them: for this is the law and the prophets.

Matthew 7:12

And whosoever shall offend one of these little ones that believe in me, it is better for him that a millstone were hanged about his neck, and he were cast into the sea.

Mark 9:42

Reason #3 What do I do if I fail?

We will fail sometimes, and there is only one thing to do. Ask forgiveness. Confess to your Father in heaven, and confess to your children. There is nothing nobler than a parent getting on the level of his child and saying, "I'm sorry. I handled that wrong. I shouldn't have said that. Will you forgive me?" This does not belittle you or your authority. You will only grow bigger in your child's eyes. Be brave enough to admit you are wrong.

And so...

If we can get over our fears, and ask YHVH to help us to be the best parent we can be, why shouldn't we then tell our children that we are trying our best? As I thought about this, I wondered what a child's response would be. Could we write a contract that lists what we are trying to do as a parent, and sign it in front of our child? If we hung it on the wall so everyone could see, would it demonstrate our love for our child? Would it be helpful to evaluate our parenting skills on a regular basis? I know incredible things would happen in our families.

Will you join me and many other families? My husband and I have signed a contract to be the best parents we can be to our seven children, ages 12 years down to eight months. We are not always the parents we should be. But, we understand the importance of the job. We want to follow YHVH's example. He made a covenant with His children and has kept that covenant for thousands of years. He knew we would fail Him repeatedly, yet He made the covenant anyway. What great love! What commitment! What a wonderful example to follow!

What we set out to do is no small task. We will be vulnerable. We will be held accountable. Our children may respond negatively. But things often get worse before they get better. That is often the way of progress. Before we embark on this task, a warning is necessary. Satan hates families. He really hates families that try to live according to Torah and all of Scripture. He will attack whenever an effort is made to build up the family. To be forewarned is to be forearmed.

Be sober, be vigilant; because your adversary the devil, as a roaring lion, walketh about, seeking whom he may devour.

I Peter 5:8

I'd like to share an excerpt from my journal as I first set out to write this book. As I continue to share with you the process of signing a ketubah for your children, I hope your heart will be the same.

"I am very humbled as I write this. Every word that has gone on these pages was accompanied by a pang in my heart. Why was I impatient last week when I was dealing with another mess made by one of my children? How will I ever accomplish my goals as a parent? How could I have thought that awful thing about my child? I am not a perfect mom, and if you ask me on the wrong day, I wouldn't even call myself a very good mom. But I love my children. I want to do right by them. I am writing this as my own heart cry. I want to get beyond mediocre how-to books to reach the heart of my children. I want to love my children with all my heart. I need to be constantly reminded of the important task I have been given as a parent. It is time to stop surviving and start thriving. I want to go beyond fixing meals and keeping little hands busy. My desire is to leave a spiritual legacy for my children, which they will pass on to their children. Will you join me so I won't be alone on this incredibly daunting journey? YHVH help and bless us all."

And He shall turn the heart of the fathers to the children, and the heart of the children to their fathers, lest I come and smite the earth with a curse.

Malachi 4:6

Notes

Chapter 2

The Ketubah

But this shall be the covenant that I will make with the house of Israel; After those days, saith the LORD, I will put my law (Torah) in their inward parts, and write it in their hearts; and will be their God, and they shall be my people.

Jeremiah 31:33

In this chapter, we will look at an actual covenant between a parent and their child. There are two different ketubahs presented, one for girls and one for boys. In Scripture, the difference between male and female is quite distinct. Raising a son is very different from raising a daughter. I have three daughters and four sons, and they are definitely different from each other. I have tried to reflect that in the two ketubahs. Each statement covers a different aspect of parenting, but they all overlap and build on each other.

As you study the different parts of the ketubah, be sure to do the action steps. They will help you to begin putting your good parenting intentions into action. You will also find space after each statement to write down your thoughts and study notes. Remember that this makes a great group study. I recommend one statement per study, with time for discussion, and time between meetings to work on the action steps.

On to the ketubahs.....

For Daughters

We love you.

YHVH formed you in the womb. He made you beautiful and smart.

We want the very best for you and we are so happy you are part of our family.

We are not perfect parents, but we promise to do our very best.

We will pray for you.

We will listen to you.

We will be a living example of how to walk in Torah, teach it to you, and show you how to study it on your own.

We will lovingly discipline you when you do wrong, to keep you on the right track. We will restore you after the discipline.

We will enjoy you and learn about you as a unique special young lady, and help you develop the talents your Heavenly Father gave you.

We will be available to help you with decisions, including the choice of your future husband, life work, and ministry.

From Mom:

I will show you how to be a good future wife by being one now.

I will patiently show you how to be a capable young lady.

From Dad:

I will meet your needs, spiritually, emotionally, and physically.

I will provide a safe haven for you to grow up in.

We hope you will return our love with your own, demonstrated by honor and obedience. But we will love you no matter what.

When we fail in any of the things listed above, we will apologize and make it right.

For Sons

We love you.

YHVH formed you in the womb. He made you handsome and smart.

We want the very best for you and we are so happy you are part of our family.

We are not perfect parents, but we promise to do our very best.

We will pray for you.

We will listen to you.

We will be a living example of how to walk in Torah, teach it to you, and show you how to study it on your own.

We will lovingly discipline you when you do wrong, to keep you on the right track. We will restore you after the discipline.

We will enjoy you and learn about you as a unique special young man, and help you develop the talents your Heavenly Father gave you.

We will be available to help you with decisions, including the choice of your future wife, life work, and ministry.

From Mom:

I will teach you about godly women and strange women. I will nurture you and build you up in your journey to manhood.

From Dad:

I will teach you to defend the innocent and stand for Torah.

I will show you how to love and respect the women in your life.

I will patiently show you the skills you will need as a man.

We hope you will return our love with your own, demonstrated by honor and obedience. But we will love you no matter what.

When we fail in any of the things listed above, we will apologize and make it right.

Let's look at each of these statements. How do we apply each one and what does Scripture have to say about them? First, let's look at the ones for both boys and girls, and then look at the gender specific ones.

We love you.

This must be our foundation. Our children must know, without a doubt, that we love them. It must be unconditional love that doesn't stop when the child misbehaves. Writing "I love you" at the top of the ketubah is not enough. We must live it out every day.

But what is love? In modern society, love is a very misunderstood word. It is used towards everything from songs to hamburgers. We can supposedly fall in and out of love, as if it were a hole in the ground. True love is much more than an emotion. It is not fluffy or red with ruffles. It is not expressed with chocolate. Love is not glamorous, but steady and reliable.

My Dad defines love as a choice. It is a choice to put the other person first. No matter what, we will demonstrate to that person that they have worth, that they are valued, and that we want what is best for them. In our family, we serve the children first at mealtime. We give out bedtime kisses. We try to stop and listen when a child is speaking. But we also discipline them when they do wrong. We want to save them from future consequences that will be far worse. This is just as much love as the good night kisses.

My husband defines love to a child as T-I-M-E. Spend time with your children. Know their interests and include them in your interests. Forget quality time; just give them quantity time. They don't evaluate the time spent with you, they just want more of it. It doesn't need to be fun time, either. Include them in your chores so they feel valuable and important. You can't show love to someone if you don't spend time with them.

The best example and how-to manual of love is the Torah, the first five books of the Bible. YHVH instructs us in the Torah to love our neighbor as ourselves. He then tells us to help our neighbor with their burdens. We are to care for widows and orphans. When we find a lost item, we return it to the owner. We keep our home safe so no one gets hurt. We show respect for other people's property. All these ideas are clearly taught in the Torah, and are just as relevant when showing love to our children as they are when loving our neighbors. By the way, if they sound like New Testament ideas to you, it's because the New Testament writers knew Torah and simply kept teaching it in their writings.

How do we use these Torah principles to show unconditional love to our children? We help them when they are struggling with an assignment or project. We return a lost item to them when we find it. We protect them in a safe environment and promote good health. We allow them to have property to call their own so they can learn about property rights. Torah is our road map, and parenting begins with love. As we explore the rest of the statements in the ketubah, we will see Torah and love at play in each one.

When we love our children, it must be unconditional. It is easy to slip into a form of conditional love without realizing it. We start putting conditions on our love. We'll demonstrate love if they clean their room. We'll treat them with respect if they first speak respectfully to us. If they misbehave, we put them on our bad list. We only offer affection if they comply with a list of rules. I don't think this is ever done intentionally. We haven't stopped loving our child, but we have stopped communicating it to them. They can begin to feel that our love must be earned and they will fear that they will never measure up. This is a tough thing to avoid, but to be forewarned is to be forearmed. Our children will disappoint and frustrate us, but we must find ways to still communicate love to them.

I saw a wonderful example of unconditional love in an article I read some time ago. The author, a mom, decided to serve her children breakfast every Friday morning. She set out the fancy tableware, made a fancy meal, and did all the cleaning up. It was simply her gift to her children, no strings attached. She showed unconditional love to her children without expectations, and was eventually rewarded with her children desiring to serve her and each other. What a wonderful example!

We often make mistakes and mess things up, even as adults, but YHVH shows amazing and unconditional love to us. We would do well to show this same love to our children. It takes intentional rethinking of our actions and intentions. We must fill our minds with the example YHVH gives us in His Word.

Bless the LORD, O my soul; and all that is within me, bless his holy name.

Bless the LORD, O my soul, and forget not all his benefits:

Who forgiveth all thine iniquities; who healeth all thy diseases;

Who redeemeth thy life from destruction; who crowneth thee with lovingkindness and tender mercies;

Who satisfieth thy mouth with good things; so that thy youth is renewed like the eagle's.

The LORD executeth righteousness and judgment for all that are oppressed.

He made known his ways unto Moses, his acts unto the children of Israel.

The LORD is merciful and gracious, slow to anger, and plenteous in mercy.

He will not always chide: neither will he keep his anger forever.

He hath not dealt with us after our sins; nor rewarded us according to our iniquities.

For as the heaven is high above the earth, so great is his mercy toward them that fear him.

As far as the east is from the west, so far hath he removed our transgressions from us.

Like as a father pitieth his children, so the LORD pitieth them that fear him.

For he knoweth our frame; he remembereth that we are dust.

As for man, his days are as grass: as a flower of the field, so he flourisheth.

For the wind passeth over it, and it is gone; and the place thereof shall know it no more.

But the mercy of the LORD is from everlasting to everlasting upon them that fear him, and his righteousness unto children's children;

To such as keep his covenant, and to those that remember his commandments to do them.

Psalm 103:1-18

We show unconditional love to our children as YHVH shows unconditional love to us.

Actions

Study I Corinthians 13, the love chapter. Come up with concrete examples of showing love to your children.

Learn the 613 commands given in the Torah. Some apply to only priests or only men, etc.

Notes

_____

_____

_____

_____

_____

_____

_____

_____

_____

_____

_____

_____

_____

_____

_____

_____

YHVH formed you in the womb. He made you beautiful, or handsome, and smart.

I will praise thee; for I am fearfully and wonderfully made: marvelous are thy works; and that my soul knoweth right well.

My substance was not hid from thee, when I was made in secret, and curiously wrought in the lowest parts of the earth.

Thine eyes did see my substance, yet being unperfect; and in thy book all my members were written, which in continuance were fashioned, when as yet there were none of them.

Psalm 139:14-16

Your child was made just right. Your child is beautiful. Look at your child as being fearfully and wonderfully made. Why am I saying this? Because sometimes we get frustrated with our children. Sometimes we ask ourselves, "What is wrong with them?" We need a fresh perspective. We need to be reminded that YHVH made our child just right. Yes, they need work and training, but look into their eyes and see what YHVH sees. Look at what they can become. They are a diamond in the rough. Show them that they are just as valuable as a diamond to you.

What if your child has special needs, or a serious disability? I understand how you can feel a bit confused at this point if you have a child with special needs. I have two children with special needs and it was and is a struggle. I literally went through the five stages of grief. I cried. I got frustrated. I didn't understand. But YHVH eventually showed me that they were formed according to His design. My children have unique struggles, but they also have unique gifts. I know that YHVH has big plans for them, and He has worked amazing things in my own life because of them.

It is not my job to decide who my children will be. It is YHVH's job, and He is very good at it. It is my job to love my children unconditionally and appreciate them for the wonderful and amazing little people they are. It is my job to build them up and support them where they are weak. It is my job to boost their confidence by reminding them that YHVH designed them and they are valuable.

As I struggled to make sense of the issues my children were facing, YHVH brought along a fellow believer who quoted one verse to me. It helped me to have peace that YHVH has the perfect plans for each of us, and I hope it will do the same for you.

And the LORD said unto him, Who hath made man's mouth? Or who maketh the dumb, or deaf, or the seeing or the blind? Have not I the LORD?

Exodus 4:11

You may recognize this verse from Moses' dealings with YHVH at the burning bush. Moses had some sort of speech impediment, but YHVH was quick to remind Moses that He not only knew about it, but had in fact put it there. He has a plan for each of us, and often, He capitalizes on our weaknesses.

And he said unto me, "My grace is sufficient for thee: for my strength is made perfect in weakness." Most gladly therefore will I rather glory in my infirmities, that the power of Christ may rest upon me.

2 Corinthians 12:9

Whether our children are super gifted or struggling to learn to talk, they were designed by our Heavenly Father, and He has wonderful plans for them. We, as parents, need to grasp this wonderful truth for our children.

Actions

Study Psalm 139.

Post pictures of your children around the house, to remind you in the heat of the moment just how precious they are.

Notes

_____

_____

_____

_____

_____

_____

_____

_____

_____

_____

_____

_____

_____

_____

_____

_____

_____

We want the very best for you and we are so happy you are part of our family.

For I know the thoughts that I think toward you, saith the LORD, thoughts of peace, and not of evil, to give you an expected end.

Jeremiah 29:11

Train up a child in the way he should go: and when he is old, he will not depart from it.

Proverbs 22:6

I am come that they might have life, and that they might have it more abundantly.

John 10:10

YHVH has wonderful plans for us as His children. He wants us to have meaningful, fulfilling lives. He has a job for each of us to do. Our job as parents is to encourage our children to find out what YHVH wants them to do, and enable them to do it. We can't have our own plans for our children, but must do our best to prepare them for what may lie ahead.

Many parents in the Bible did a beautiful job of this. I think of Jochebed, Moses' mother, who taught him the ways of the Hebrews and the promise of deliverance from Egypt. How exciting that he would be the tool to bring that deliverance! Hannah taught her son, Samuel, to honor and obey YHVH. Later, when YHVH spoke to him directly, Samuel was ready to listen.

Our job is to lay aside our hopes and dreams for our children, and prepare our children to embrace the work YHVH has for them. We can be confident that He has great and wonderful plans for them.

Each child in our family should also feel like an integral part of the family team. What your family does, they should do together. Chores and projects should be shared. Even the smallest child can hold tools or help wipe the table off. They quickly learn that their contributions help family life to run more smoothly.

Tough times need to be shared, too. I remember my Dad losing his job when I was younger. We all prayed together and helped Dad look for another job. I even helped him type his resume. When we don't share our struggles with our children, they worry unnecessarily because they can sense that something is wrong. They are also blocked from learning how to handle trials properly. Keep things age-appropriate, of course, but do your best to help each member of the family feel like part of the team.

Actions

Study Exodus 2:1-10 and I Samuel 1:1-2:11 to learn more about Jochebed and Hannah.

Play games and do chores together as a team. Come up with a team name.

Find out what visions your children have. YHVH may already be pointing them in a certain direction.

Notes

_____

_____

_____

_____

_____

_____

_____

_____

_____

_____

_____

_____

_____

_____

_____

_____

We are not perfect parents, but we promise to do our best.

This concept, in essence, is what this book is all about. We are not perfect parents. For some reason, YHVH chose to give children to less than perfect parents. I don't know why, but I have to believe that He knows best. Sometimes I feel that I learn more from my children than my children learn from me. That may be part of His plan.

But the essential point is that I need help. I get busy fixing meals and settling fights and washing clothes, and I forget how important my job is. I have been given a little person, a soul, to care for and raise. The things they learn while in my care will stay with them for the rest of their lives.

Yes, ultimately they will stand on their own two feet. They will have to answer for their own choices and we cannot force them down a certain path. But our influence cannot be underestimated. We must realize our position in the molding of a life. This ketubah is designed to be a constant reminder of our job and our delight as their parent. We need to be reminded, at least I do.

It sounds rather scary and overwhelming. Praise YHVH that He only requires our best. Being lax and irresponsible is unacceptable, but He doesn't require perfection either. He simply wants us to take this job seriously, and with the help of the Holy Spirit, give it our very best shot.

I have heard it said many times, "Courage is not the absence of fear. It is the belief that there is something more important than fear." We all have fears and uncertainties as we parent, but we can rise above them with YHVH's help.

Here's a blog post I wrote that summarizes perfectly:

"I enjoy spending some time on pinterest occasionally. I love looking at the delicious prepared meals and the perfectly decorated rooms. Many bloggers also have a wonderful ability to get lovely photographs, you know, the ones where their children are immaculate and dressed in coordinating outfits. It's easy to look at these staged photos and assume that they represent actual life on the other side of the computer screen. As a result, we can end up crippled with feelings of inferiority. We know we can never achieve what they have done, so we are tempted to give up trying. Wouldn't it be so much easier if everyone posted polaroids instead? What if we only saw candid shots from life in other people's homes?

I have a feeling that if we only saw candid photos, we would soon discover that everyone has struggles. We would find people with financial struggles, insecurities, special needs children, dirty dishes, health problems, and even character flaws! YHVH created us all different, with different gifts and weaknesses, different circumstances and struggles, and yet, He is there with each of us to help us along the way. None of us is exempt from the darker side of life, but we do have YHVH along side us.

Next time you see that magazine quality living room photo, or the picture of children that have never seen a mud puddle, remember that behind that photo is a family that also struggles in their own way. Take each day that YHVH gives you, with its struggles and blessings, and do your best with it. Be thankful that your life is candid. Everyone would be afraid to sit down in that perfect living room anyway. And life is much more interesting with mud puddles!"

Actions

Read the book of Joshua, for an example of courage in action
and Philippians 4:13, since we all need reminding that our
strength comes from YHVH.

Notes

_____

_____

_____

_____

_____

_____

_____

_____

_____

_____

_____

_____

_____

_____

_____

_____

_____

We will pray for you.

What we cannot do, YHVH can. Where we are inconsistent or forgetful, He can fill in the gap. But we need to be talking to Him and asking Him for help.

We are to pray in faith, knowing that He hears us. Once I got a grasp on this concept, it revolutionized the way I pray. If I truly believe that YHVH will hear me and answer, then I don't need to worry or fret. How can I be confident that He will answer? Pray for those things that He promised to do in Scripture, using the Scripture as you pray. How do I know what He promised? I would suggest jotting down promises as you read.

There are so many promises in Scripture that I will not attempt to make a list here. But let's look at Psalm 127.

Except the LORD build the house, they labour in vain that build it: except the LORD keep the city, the watchman walketh but in vain.

It is vain for you to rise up early, to sit up late, to eat the bread of sorrows: for so he giveth his beloved sleep.

Lo, children are an heritage of the LORD: and the fruit of the womb is his reward.

As arrows are in the hand of a mighty man: so are children of the youth.

Happy is the man that hath his quiver full of them: they shall not be ashamed, but they shall speak with the enemies in the gate.

Psalm 127

YHVH says that our children are an inheritance or a heritage. We can pray that our children will truly be a blessing, a reward, and inheritance. We can pray that they will be a joy to us.

In these verses, our children are compared to arrows. Arrows are supposed to hit their target. We can pray that our children become all that YHVH intends them to be. We can pray for them to be successful and fruitful.

YHVH says that having many children is a blessing. We can pray for more children to raise for Him.

YHVH promises to give us sleep. We, as parents, tend to worry about our children, and for me, it can be worse at night. But when I realize that YHVH promised to do the watching for me, I can rest easy. I can pray for His watchful protection over my family.

There are many promises like these in Scripture. It's your job and privilege to find them. Psalms is a great place to start. However, there is one thing that will get in the way of our prayers. That thing is our sin. If we have unconfessed sin in our heart, He will not hear. First, check your life for sin, and repent. Then go confidently to Him in prayer on behalf of your children. Just a note to consider, unforgiveness towards others is a big hindrance to your prayers being answered. We are to forgive others as He forgave us.

I have often prayed over my children while they are asleep in bed at night. I enjoy the quiet and can reflect on each child and their needs. It has become a special time for me as a mother to lift them up in prayer. I also thank Him for answering my prayer, knowing that He will. I would encourage you to find a special time or place to pray for your children regularly.

Actions

Begin a promise notebook to jot down promises in Scripture as you come across them. You can pray for these things confidently, knowing He will hear you and keep His promise.

Study the Psalms, which are, in essence, a collection of prayers. Learn to pray with the honesty and trust that the Psalmists did.

Consider praying the Amidah, a daily prayer. It is firmly rooted in Scripture and will help you to have a humble and worshipful approach before our King.

Notes

_____

_____

_____

_____

_____

_____

_____

_____

_____

_____

_____

_____

We will listen to you.

It is very easy to do all the talking as the parent. "Because I said so" becomes our mantra. "Listen up" and "Be quiet" both come out of our mouths regularly. Well, at least they may come out of my mouth. We have gotten the idea that we are the only ones in the parent/child relationship that have something important to say.

My friends, that ought not to be. I am trying to develop the habit of stopping and listening to my children. Just pause and look your children in the eye when they are talking. They will help you understand them. With a little encouragement, they will tell you what has been bothering them. Sometimes my children have attitude problems. I invite them up into my lap and ask them how we can fix the situation. Usually the problem is easily remedied, because I took the time to listen.

If I am to enter into a covenant relationship with my child, the relationship needs to be two-way. My child needs to know that their opinion matters. Children don't have the final say, because they lack the wisdom and experience. However, the ability to think through a problem, form an opinion, and share it with someone you trust is important for a child to develop. They should feel safe coming to us with their thoughts, fears, worries, hopes and dreams. They may even come to us with a sin that they need to confess, but only if they know we will listen without ridicule or rejection. We foster this relationship as we make a habit of listening to them every day.

Remember that our best example of parenting skills is the way our Heavenly Father parents us. He listens to us when we pray, and often answers us before we pray. He wants to hear from each of us individually. He enjoys the unique approach each of us has. We as parents should enjoy listening to our children just as much.

Each of my children has a special way of communicating with me. My son jabbers nonstop. My daughter likes to be very private and whisper. Embrace each one for who they are and strive to really understand them by listening.

I once heard a story of two little boys playing in the sandbox with their trucks, while their mothers visited inside. As is often the case, a fight broke out between the boys. Trucks were swiped, angry words flung carelessly, and more than little feelings were hurt. But one boy was pierced in his conscience, and wanted to make things right. He wanted to apologize to the other boy, but couldn't seem to get it right. So he went to his mother for help. But as he stood in the kitchen in front of his mother, tears streaming down his dirty face, and sand trickling out of the toy truck, she could only see the mess, and sent him away.

When we do not listen to our children, we lose opportunities to teach them. We lose their trust. We lose their interest. Ultimately, we lose their hearts. We must take time to listen to them, whether it's trivial in our eyes or not. Nothing is trivial to them, and when we listen to them about the little things, they will come to us with the big things.

Actions

Read some Psalms. Notice that YHVH listens to us, even when our prayers are less than perfect. We can follow His example with our children.

Spend today looking for opportunities to listen to your child. Remember to look at them and really pay attention.

Notes

_____

_____

_____

_____

_____

_____

_____

_____

_____

_____

_____

_____

_____

_____

_____

_____

We will be a living example of how to walk in Torah, teach it, and show you how to study it on your own.

Many parents understand the importance of being a good example to their children. However, why should they be an example of Torah specifically? Isn't the law done away with? The answer may surprise you.

First, the word Torah does not mean law. Torah refers to the first five books of the Bible, and also conveys the concept of instructions for living. YHVH created the world and knows how it works and how to enjoy the blessings. His "commands" are equal to the law of gravity. You cannot alter basic laws of physics like gravity, and you cannot alter His commands. Those who obey what He says are blessed, but those who try to change or defy His commands will lose the blessings. Obedience brings promises of peace, health, family, and long life, because these promises are inevitable. All of Scripture teaches us how to live right, but Torah is the foundation. Once you have a grasp of Torah and what it teaches, you will see that the rest of Scripture has its roots in Torah. The same concepts are taught, but may be expounded upon or taught from a different angle.

If we want to live a blessed life, we need to follow the principles taught in the first five books of the Bible. If we want our children to live blessed lives, we need to teach them to do the same. There are no shortcuts. We need to fill our minds and hearts with Torah and begin to live it. As our children watch our example and systematically learn Torah, they will be blessed also.

> *If we want to live a blessed life, we need to follow the principles taught in the first five books of the Bible.*

Torah is not a curse. For example, celebrating the Shabbat rest every Saturday brings balance to our lives. It has built-in stress control as we set aside the cares of work, household duties and responsibilities and choose to spend the day reading and studying Scripture, fellow shipping with family and friends, and simply resting. It's like getting seven weeks of vacation every year. Keeping the commands brings blessing. As we teach our children Torah through our example, we are giving them the gifts and blessings that Torah provides.

Torah was not done away with. Yeshua came to earth and gave us a perfect example of how to live out Torah. He showed love to His neighbors, which included publicans and sinners. He kept Shabbat by listening to the Torah reading in the synagogue each week. He brought the proper sacrifices to the temple (which we currently cannot do.) When it appears that He was attacking a command, He was referring to religious rules invented by the religious leaders of the day. He wanted them to return to simply following Scripture, not man-made laws.

I would encourage you to learn, study, and live Torah yourself, then pass it on to your children through your example and instruction. Discuss Torah principles as situations arise. If they come to you with a squabble or fight, ask them what Torah says. Before long, they will respond with, "Treat others the way you want to be treated." Teach them how to study it for themselves as they grow older. You will be amazed at the blessings.

Actions

Begin reading the weekly Torah portion with your family. You will find a schedule in the back of this book.

Don't underestimate your children. There are some great child friendly Torah portions out there, including a book I wrote. I encourage you to use these. But also remember that with training and instruction, they can listen to and understand the Torah directly from Scripture.

Notes

_____

_____

_____

_____

_____

_____

_____

_____

_____

_____

_____

_____

_____

_____

_____

We will lovingly discipline you when you do wrong, to keep you on the right track. We will restore you after the discipline.

But I love my child too much to discipline them, you may say. I completely understand this thought. I have thought it often myself. My child might be throwing a fit, and I just want to calm them down and make everything all right. But that is not what is best for the child. Let's remember that true unconditional love always does what is best for the other person. If I allowed my child to throw a fit, I am reinforcing their selfishness. I am giving them a tremendous disadvantage when they get out in the world and relate to other people. They will have a very difficult time learning to exhibit true love, which is the heart of Torah. Unfortunately, while blessings come with obedience, cursings come with disobedience. If we want our child to enjoy blessings throughout life, and avoid the curses and negative consequences, we must teach them to obey and discipline them when they don't obey.

But curses for disobedience sound very harsh, you say. YHVH is not shooting lightning bolts at us when we do wrong. But He made the world, and He understands that you will reap what you sow. He made you and loves you, and wants what is best for you. He knows that if you eat a poisonous mushroom, your life will be drastically shortened. The commands in Torah are for our own protection. He knows that if you eat unclean meats such as pork and shellfish, you are consuming all the filth that the animal consumed. He sees the danger, and has warned us with His commands. YHVH is not a brutal, mean God. But sin is a brutal, mean taskmaster. It will destroy us every time. YHVH simply wants to protect us from the inevitable consequences for sin.

> *True unconditional love always does what is best for the other person.*

We, as parents, are asked to do the same for our children. We are to teach them the commands and warn them of the dangers. When they do not obey, we need to punish them to save them from a worse fate. Punishment is unpleasant for a few minutes, but it is much preferred to a life lived outside the safety and wisdom of YHVH's commands. Discipline is much more than punishment. It is training, teaching, modeling, preparing for a life of obedience and blessing. Be sure to balance any needed punishment with positive reinforcement. As your child grows, so should your explanations of why we need to make certain choices. When discipline is a lifestyle of training, rather than an event, it is much more effective.

When we discipline, methodology is not as important as love and consistency. Many parenting books are a dime a dozen, promising a magical way to get your kids to behave once and for all. But there is no magical way. Dealing with their disobedience and praising their obedience consistently is the key. When you have to punish your children, please take the time to restore them afterward. Give them a hug. Reassure them that all is forgiven. Talk to them about how to do better next time. Pray with them. Help them make restitution if it is needed. Dealing with sin is no fun for anyone, but it is essential to help your child stay on the right track.

Keep your word to your children. This goes for promises, but it also applies to punishment. If you say that they will not get a special treat if they don't sit still and wait, that is exactly what must happen. In order to effectively keep your word, you must be in control of your emotions. If you remain calm and simply do what you say, your children will benefit from your consistency. However, if you lose control of your emotions, your children now have the control. They can manipulate you if they know they can get an emotional response. Torah commands are black and white, and your rules must be the same. Once again, YHVH gives us the perfect parenting example through His methods with us.

Actions

Study Deuteronomy 28, Proverbs 22:6, I John 1:9 and Exodus 20.

Make a list of house rules, but keep them short so everyone can remember them.

Notes

_____

_____

_____

_____

_____

_____

_____

_____

_____

_____

_____

_____

_____

_____

_____

_____

We will enjoy you and learn about you as a unique special child, and help you develop the talents your Heavenly Father gave you.

This is the fun part of parenting. It's not very hard to cherish our children as individuals, and enjoy their unique personalities. I have a prima donna/second momma who adores raising ducks. I have a tomboy who loves to climb trees and explore, but is also a wonderful artist and dancer. I have a young man who likes to spar with his Daddy, and gives hugs to me. The younger ones are still trying to find their place and their interests, but I see the beginnings.

Cultivate their interests and let them have hobbies. Just don't try to force your own interests on them. We are all unique and that is what makes the world beautiful. Your child was created with special abilities and gifts. Help them develop their talents, rather than projecting your own expectations on them.

Actions

Examine some snowflakes together with your children. It will give you both an appreciation for our Creator's creativity and the beauty of being unique.

Make hand prints or fingerprint pictures to celebrate your child's uniqueness.

Provide an abundance of opportunities for your children, so they can find their niche in life.

Notes

_____

_____

_____

_____

_____

_____

_____

_____

_____

_____

_____

_____

_____

_____

We will be available to help you with decisions, including the choice of your future spouse, life work, and ministry.

I have not helped my children pick out a spouse, but my parents helped me pick out mine. I was happy to have my parents' help, and even dependent on it. Why? Because I had developed the habit of seeking my parents' help with the little things. It was only natural for me to depend on their wisdom for such a big decision.

They did not make the decision for me. They did provide feedback and wisdom. They gave us accountability by always being there. They gave us opportunity to get to know each other. When we made the decision to get married, they blessed us.

Looking back, I would suggest that parents set the stage for this big decision when their children are very young. Teach your children what qualities to look for in a spouse. Encourage them to pray for the right spouse. Gently guide them through little decisions, showing them the value of many counselors. Lay the groundwork early, and the process will be a lot easier later on.

When that possible spouse presents himself or herself, talk to your son or daughter often throughout the process. Find out what they like and don't like, what concerns them. Please remember that this is the worst time in the world to force your authority. They are on the threshold of adulthood, but also may desire the protection of Mom and Dad. They may need you to give them a safe way to exit an undesirable relationship. Sometimes a guy comes along that a girl really doesn't want to pursue. Let Daddy handle it. My sister had this happen once. She told him to talk to her Dad. He never showed up.

If your children feel safe in your relationship, they will readily seek your advice and counsel, and sometimes your protection. They will be anxious to please you. You are their guide, and shouldn't just declare what they should do. They need to own this decision. By the way, there is no Prince Charming or beautiful princess. You simply work with your child to make the best decision, bathe the whole thing in prayer, bless them, and encourage them to keep their vows no matter what.

The choice of a spouse is not the only decision to make. Your children will spend most of their life in adulthood. They will have ministry opportunities, and a job. You can be a source of counsel and guidance for them. Most girls will have the blessing of staying at home and raising a family. Help them to see the tremendous importance and value of this job. It is just as important as bringing home the paycheck. Teach your children to look for opportunities to serve. Help them to recognize when to say yes to these opportunities, and when to say no, because it would be too much for them to take on.

I would encourage you to find the balance when helping your children with decisions. Don't make the decisions for them, but don't leave them to make the decisions alone. Think of yourself as a guide. The entrance into adulthood was a beautiful time in my life, and with some work in advance, it can be beautiful for your children, too.

Actions

Teach your child desirable qualities in a spouse. Start by making a written list of those qualities.

Work with them as a team to make smaller decisions.

Give them ministry opportunities, such as mission trips and service projects.

Notes

_____

_____

_____

_____

_____

_____

_____

_____

_____

_____

_____

_____

_____

_____

_____

We hope you will return our love with your own, demonstrated by honor and obedience. But we will love you no matter what.

Have you read the book of Hosea lately? YHVH told Hosea to marry a harlot. She was consistently unfaithful to him and sinned openly, to the point that he had to buy her out of the slave trade. He was told to be faithful to her and love her no matter what. Hosea gives us a beautiful picture of our Heavenly Father's unending love for us. We stumble and fall, on an hourly basis at times, but He is always faithful. He asks us to love our children the same way.

Oh, I do love my children like that, you may say. Were you feeling the love when they broke something of yours? How about when they told you they hated you, or threw a fit in the store? This is where the rubber meets the road. You need to have the ability to see past the situation and do what is best for the child, even in the face of rejection or obnoxious behavior. This is a very tall order, and can only be done with supernatural help. This is, again, the crucial point. We cannot succeed as parents in our own strength. We must go to our Heavenly Father and ask for help, again and again and again. He is faithful to help us, even when all is against us, humanly speaking.

When a child does reject you by saying, "I hate you," etc., it is important not to force things. They are just acting in the heat of the moment. Love cannot be forced. It is freely given and thus more worth the earning. Remember that words are often thrown around in the heat of the moment. Don't reject your children; rather, remain consistent and steadfast.

> *We must go to our Heavenly Father and ask for help, again and again and again.*

The best move to make is to leave your child in your Heavenly Father's hands. He knows them inside and out, and He is in the business of restoration, even in the big mistakes and sins your child may commit. He made a covenant with us, and we have rejected Him many times. Yet, He has promised to restore all things. Praise YHVH! He can do the same in your family and in mine.

Actions

Read the book of Hosea. He is a type of Yeshua, the ultimate
restorer. How can you follow his example as a parent?

Notes

_____

_____

_____

_____

_____

_____

_____

_____

_____

_____

_____

_____

_____

_____

_____

_____

_____

_____

_____

When I fail in any of the things listed above, I will apologize and make it right.

If we can get this one thing right, we are bound to be successful parents. If we get this one thing wrong, many other areas of parenting just won't hold true. Pride is the first sin in the Proverbs list of abominable sins. It ruins everything and tends to recruit other sins to protect itself.

These six things doth the LORD hate: yea, seven are abomination unto him:

A proud look, a lying tongue, and hands that shed innocent blood,

An heart that deviseth wicked imaginations, feet that be swift in running to mischief,

A false witness that speaketh lies, and he that soweth discord among brethren.

Proverbs 6:16-19

The only way to combat pride is to stop thinking about yourself. Living in humility means that it is all about the other person. When you choose to put your child first, it is not important whether you are right or not. You just want to see them growing and learning. When you make a mistake, you will naturally desire to make it right.

The only way to combat pride is to stop thinking about yourself.

Pride, however, demands that you look good at the expense of the other person. Pride prevents you from apologizing, because you would look less than perfect. Pride reminds me of the roosters in our backyard. They puff up the feathers around their neck so it looks like a big collar. They circle each other, bouncing around, trying to look bigger. They crow and fly at each other, flapping their wings for effect. They look big for a minute, but before long, they are a bloody mess, pitiful, stained and scarred. This is what pride does to us. It leaves us and our loved ones in a bloody mess. However, a humble apology is a balm to heal our emotional wounds.

This is particularly true in the parent/child relationship. Our children are little people, and should be treated as such. Too often, they simply get ordered around, told what to do, and instructed to wait. But they can be hurt and feel frustrated. We ought to treat them kindly, and when we fail, apologize to them, just as we would to an adult. Will you put your child first? You will have to leave the pride in the dust. Repent, and decide that pride will no longer be a part of your life. YHVH will help you, and your children will love you even more.

Actions

Look up pride, humility, and confession in a concordance. Write down the definitions and find verses that illustrate each concept.

Get a good mental picture of a proud man and a humble man. Do you really want to look like a beaten rooster.

Notes

_____

_____

_____

_____

_____

_____

_____

_____

_____

_____

_____

_____

_____

_____

_____

For the Girls

I will patiently show you how to be a capable young lady.

Moms, it's our job to teach our daughters the ways of the feminine race. We don't want them to become the strange woman! Modesty, grace and true femininity are best taught by Mom.

Girls need to be taught proper manners, modesty, and household jobs. Women have the wonderful ability to beautify their corner of the world. Let your daughters practice the womanly arts. Teach them proper baby and childcare, so they will be adept mothers. Teach them to use their power of influence wisely and prudently.

In Scripture, women have an incredibly important job with many facets. The Proverbs 31 woman managed a large household, which would have been equivalent to managing a business in our minds. She bought and sold property. She ran a business with the merchants. She possessed many creative skills. She was strong and capable. The word virtuous means powerful force. A godly woman is not a doormat, but rather she understands her potential power and uses it wisely.

A godly woman protects and surrounds her husband. A Jewish wedding ceremony demonstrates this when the bride circles the bridegroom seven times. A wife has intuition and can save the household much heartache by listening to it. She must then lovingly share her insight with her husband. She also protects her husband from the strange woman by being a faithful and endearing wife.

I feel it is best to teach all these skills in an organized way. I have listed some books in the additional resources chapter that you may find helpful.

Actions

Study Proverbs 31. Begin teaching womanly arts in an organized way.

Learn about the concept of the "ezer kenegdo," translated as helpmeet in our English Bibles. Teach these concepts to your daughters.

Notes

_____

_____

_____

_____

_____

_____

_____

_____

_____

_____

_____

_____

_____

_____

_____

_____

_____

I will show you how to be a good future wife by being one now.

Children learn from their mother's example. They learn what family life is like by watching us. What do they see when they watch you? How do you treat each other as a couple? You will teach more as you model communication skills and cooperation in everyday life than you will with a planned teaching time.

Your children will learn about respect, proper conflict resolution, the importance of apologizing, teamwork, affection, and much more. In order to give your children a head start on a great marriage, take the time to make your marriage the best it can be. Time invested with your spouse is also time invested in your children's future.

Your children should know that Mommy and Daddy are committed to each other. Sure, you may disagree sometimes, but do your children see that you apologize and make up? Do they see you playfully show affection to each other? A little kiss or a playful tickle shows your children that you enjoy each other, and that you are friends. This gives them great security, knowing that Mommy and Daddy will stick together no matter what.

Parents with excellent marriages tend to have children with excellent marriages, because they modeled the behavior needed to make things work. Take the time to be a good husband or wife, and point out casually to your children the actions you take to have a great marriage.

> *Parents with excellent marriages tend to have children with excellent marriages, because they modeled the behavior needed to make things work.*

Being a wife, specifically, is a high calling and can be a tough job. A wife is to be her husband's protector, confidant, friend, lover, and rebuker when needed. All these jobs must be done with the grace and finesse that YHVH gifted us with. When our husband succeeds, we are his biggest cheerleader. When he makes bad choices, we find a way to help him back on the straight and narrow. Our daughters need to know how to perform this awesome job when they are married. I would encourage you to study the role of a wife in Scripture together with your daughters. You will both benefit tremendously.

Actions

Invest time and study books to improve your marriage.

Spend time with each other to keep the relationship alive and fresh.

Do some Bible studies with your daughters about the role of a wife. I have included some suggested books in the resources chapter to get you started.

Notes

_____

_____

_____

_____

_____

_____

_____

_____

_____

_____

_____

_____

_____

_____

I will meet your needs, spiritually, emotionally, and physically. I will provide a safe haven for you to grow up in.

It has often been said that daughters who know their Daddy loves them have no reason to look for love elsewhere. I believe this is true because it was true for me. My Dad did not speak of love much but he showed it often. He helped me with schoolwork, played on the floor with me, and went on walks around the yard checking on trees with me. I remember seeing him restack some firewood and I asked him why. He said that he didn't want any of his girls to get hurt, so he was making sure the pile wouldn't topple over. He complimented us on our pretty dresses and gave us hugs. We knew he loved us even if he didn't say it much. All three of us made it safely to the wedding altar on our Daddy's arm.

Does your daughter know you love her? Does she see your provision for her needs? Does she feel secure because of your protection? Make an effort everyday to show her you cherish her and care about her. Are her basic needs like food and clothing provided for? Does she know you love her and does she feel safe coming to you with her problems? Are you acting as a priest in your home? Are you praying for and leading your family spiritually? Be careful to not be so caught up in providing for her financially that you are never home to meet her emotional and spiritual needs. A Daddy's love for his daughter cannot be given by anyone else.

Evaluate yourself as a dad. Are you providing for your family's physical needs? Pray for YHVH to bless your efforts. Are you connecting with them emotionally? Take the time to just listen to them. This alone will do a world of good. Are you leading them spiritually? Seek YHVH's face in prayer and then use the amazing resource he gave you, your wife. She is probably eager and waiting to help you be a spiritually leader in your home.

Actions

Spend time with your daughter. Consider daddy/daughter outings, but don't overlook the little things like reading stories with her.

Notes

_____

_____

_____

_____

_____

_____

_____

_____

_____

_____

_____

_____

_____

_____

_____

_____

For the boys

I will teach you about godly women and strange women.

This is a tall order for moms and dads and must be taught sooner than most people think. It's a tough world for boys, when even the store ads are hazardous. I have already started teaching my six-year-old son about women and still feel like I am playing catch-up.

We must teach our sons that the strange woman advertises her body, but she is like a spider, setting a trap for them. She only wants to destroy them. She must be avoided at all costs. Proverbs talks much about the strange woman. Help your son recognize warning signs in her behavior and teach him to steer clear. Our sons need to be able to quickly identify the strange woman and run the other way, as Joseph did with Potiphar's wife.

The godly woman, on the other hand, conceals her body and dresses modestly. She behaves appropriately. A modest woman tends to be more trustworthy. As Proverbs tells us, she is of great price, and worthy to be a bride. We need to teach our sons to value such women, and treat them with respect. Does that mean we teach them to disrespect the strange woman? Not at all. But they should be taught to keep their dealings with the strange woman as brief as possible.

Make a game of it at a young age. When at the store, try to find modestly dressed women, and point out that they are dressed right. Make sure you and your daughters are dressed right. When you read a book together, or see women on TV, ask your sons (and daughters) if those women were behaving righteously, or creating stumbling blocks for others. Start young and make the concept of strange and godly women second nature for them.

Actions

More than anything else, start young. If you wait until you think this topic is age appropriate, it could be too late. If you are conscious of teaching your sons about the opposite race when they are five, you can teach them a little here and a little there.

Notes

_____

_____

_____

_____

_____

_____

_____

_____

_____

_____

_____

_____

_____

_____

_____

I will nurture you and build you up in your journey to manhood.

Moms have an important role in a young man's life, but they must learn balance. We tend to see our five-year-old frog-catching, tree-climbing, affectionate little boy. But as the days of scraped knees and dirty laundry flit away, he has become a young man, on the very edge of independence. We cannot continue to treat him like a five-year-old. We must encourage him on his journey to confident manhood. If we try to hold him back and continue to make decisions for him, he will rebel, resent his parents, or run. However, a loving nurturing mom can be the softness and reassurance a young man needs.

How can we begin now to prepare him for the days ahead? Make a point of providing opportunities for him to practice being a man. Ask him to use his strong hands to open a jar for you. Praise him for his bravery when he walks past a big dog that previously scared him. Take him on an errand run as your "protector." Let him "act the man" at four, and he will have no problem at twenty.

Remember, you can make or break him. Do not baby him. Instead, encourage him to stand on his own two feet. Let him make decisions, even if he sometimes makes the wrong one. We sometimes learn more from our mistakes than our successes. As you do this, you will find that he will return your efforts with an affection and respect well worth the earning. He will look at his mother as a jewel worth cherishing and protecting, not chains that need to be broken.

Actions

Read Proverbs. It is full of common sense wisdom that you will need to teach your son. I know of families that encouraged their children to memorize whole chapters of Proverbs. That was time well spent.

You may also want to provide some good reading material for your son. Horatio Alger wrote several fiction books about young men in the 1800's. They are examples of bravery, hard work, honesty, and most important, an uncanny affection for their mothers. (Not overly religious, simply moral) G.A. Henty also wrote excellent historical fiction for boys.

Notes

_____

_____

_____

_____

_____

_____

_____

_____

_____

_____

_____

_____

_____

I will teach you to defend the innocent and stand for Torah.

Dads, picture great Bible heroes like Moses, David, Joshua, Joseph, and others like Judas Maccabee. They did what was right in the eyes of YHVH. They protected the women and the children. They fought for truth. These are the kind of men we want our sons to become. How do we teach them? Read to them about these great men. Lift them up as heroes. Talk about their strengths and weaknesses. Once you explain to your boys that the battle of Jericho really happened, then imaginary heroes like Superman tend to lose their glamor. Children prefer fact to fable, hands down. My children often ask me of a story or movie, "Is it true?" If the answer is yes, then they are a captive audience.

Give your sons heroes that defend the innocent and stand for Torah, and they will do the same. Be sure to ask yourself as well, "Am I defending truth and Torah? Am I protecting the innocent, such as the members of my own family?" You can be the biggest hero in your son's life with your own example.

Actions

Read to your sons about the great Bible heroes. Encourage them to take it a step further by acting it out, or drawing their own comic book of real heroes.

Notes

_____

_____

_____

_____

_____

_____

_____

_____

_____

_____

_____

_____

_____

_____

_____

_____

_____

I will show you how to love and respect the women in your life.

Dads, love and respect the women in your life, and your son will learn to do the same. Love his mother and his sisters and his grandmother. Point out little ways to show honor to them, like opening the door, or giving impromptu hugs. Simple acts, like directing him to go give his mother a kiss, develop habits. Those habits will stay with him throughout life. If you value your wife and treat her like a million bucks, he will learn to value her, too. Real men show honor to women. They do not mistreat them, or belittle them. They do not make demands or delight in lording it over women.

Yeshua showed great respect to women. He honored His mother by turning the water into wine at the wedding. He talked to the woman at the well in John 4, which was culturally unacceptable. He honored the woman who anointed Him with ointment. While He hung on the cross, He made sure His mother would be cared for after He was gone. In Torah, women are not second-class citizens, but are cared for as jewels. Unfortunately, in most cultures throughout history, women were not honored and valued. They have been looked on as possessions, free labor, and nothing more than breeding stock. We can change that. We can teach our daughters that they have immense value, and we can teach our sons to cherish women. We can break the chain in this generation and begin following Yeshua's example.

Actions

Give your son lots of "honor practice" with his mother and sisters. It will become a habit.

Look closely at how Yeshua treated women as you read the gospels.

Notes

_____

_____

_____

_____

_____

_____

_____

_____

_____

_____

_____

_____

_____

_____

_____

_____

_____

I will patiently show you the skills you will need as a man.

Dad, your son, and often, your daughter, needs to be able to do basic woodworking, auto repair, household maintenance, hunting and butchering, home finances, basic survival skills, and many other skills. These skills, again, are best taught systematically. You need to have a list of skills that can be checked off as they master them. There are resources listed in chapter 4 that you may find helpful in accomplishing this task.

Your son will eventually be a breadwinner for his own home. He needs marketable skills as well. The face of higher education has changed dramatically in recent years. Going away to a college campus is no longer required. Apprenticeships, online college courses, and home based businesses are all legitimate options now. Be sure to pray together to determine the best course of action for your son.

Actions

Systematically teach your son the skills he needs for every day life. Some of these skills are also appropriate to teach to your daughters.

Notes

_____

_____

_____

_____

_____

_____

_____

_____

_____

_____

_____

_____

_____

_____

_____

_____

_____

As we conclude our look at each part of the ketubah, let's talk a minute about implementing it. I would recommend going through the book and praying about each section of the ketubah. If you agree on each portion, then print it up on nice paper and get a frame for it. Create an event where you read it with your children, sign it and hang it up together. Have a special meal to celebrate. In the next chapter, we will be talking more about keeping the commitment you have chosen to make.

As I was writing this chapter, my nine-year-old daughter got up out of bed. We had had a very unpleasant situation before bed with the girls mistreating their little sister. It was obvious that she was still quite bothered by it. I finally got her to talk as she curled up in my lap. We quietly talked about ways she could show love to her little sister, rather than excluding her. Then I showed her what I was writing. I read the ketubah to her, and she was quite touched. I told her that I struggle, too, and I need help to do my best.

Then I shared with her an unforgettable line from a wonderful movie, "Anne of Green Gables." "Tomorrow is always fresh, with no mistakes in it." How wonderful it is to have our sins forgiven and forgotten. She went to bed determined to show her sister love in the morning. She got a fresh start, and so did I. The past mistakes that I sometimes felt crippled by were gone. My vulnerability had changed her view of me. I was no longer a parent telling her what to do. I was a fellow traveler and sometimes I stumbled, too. I'm so glad that tomorrow is fresh for me, too.

Now, that's what parenting ought to be!

Chapter 3

Blessing our children

The LORD bless thee, and keep thee: The LORD make his face shine upon thee, and be gracious unto thee: The LORD lift up his countenance upon thee, and give thee peace.

Numbers 6:24-26

So we have made a covenant with our children. We are committed to our responsibility as parents, and we understand what those responsibilities are. But how do we maintain the accountability? How do we keep momentum?

I believe a key is found in the tradition of blessing your children on Shabbat. In Scripture, the day begins as the sun sets. Notice that in Genesis 1, it continually reads, "the evening and the morning." On Friday night, we usher in the Shabbat as the sun goes down. Many families have a special meal, and bless their children.

The foundation of blessing our children is saying the priestly blessing over our children. This blessing is found in Numbers 6:22-27.

And the LORD spake unto Moses, saying,

Speak unto Aaron and unto his sons, saying, On this wise ye shall bless the children of Israel, saying unto them,

The LORD bless thee, and keep thee:

The LORD make his face shine upon thee, and be gracious unto thee:

The LORD lift up his countenance upon thee, and give thee peace.

And they shall put my name upon the children of Israel; and I will bless them.

Numbers 6:22-27

I wouldn't call it magical, but saying this blessing is very important. As verse 27 says, when we use this blessing, YHVH promises to bless us. When a father, as the priest of the home, says this blessing over his children, it is even more powerful. If he says it in Hebrew, which is YHVH's language, there is a special thing that happens. YHVH's power is released in our life. Below is the Hebrew followed by the transliteration, or English pronunciation of the priestly blessing, so you can say it in Hebrew without needing to be able to read Hebrew.

יברכ ךיהוה וישמרך יאר יהוה פניו אליך ויחנך ישא
יהוה פניו אליך וישם לך שלום ץ

Ye-va-re-khe-kha YHVH ve-yish-me-re-kha ya-er
YHVH pa-nav e-ley-kha vi-chun-ne-kha
yi-sa YHVH pa-nav e-ley-kha ve-ya-sem
le-kha sha-lom

I have come to understand the power of this blessing partly by the attacks it gets. Friday afternoon is often the toughest part of the whole week. Satan knows that if he can get us upset with each other and rushed and busy, perhaps we will skip the blessing and just eat our dinner. When this has happened, the whole following week seemed a bit askew. We have learned to be very diligent to keep things running smoothly on Friday. We have to be alert and on guard against Satan's attacks. He hates families and he knows that preventing this blessing from being said will do some damage.

The foundation of blessing our children
is saying the priestly blessing over
our children.

I have heard of other families where the blessing was said for many years, and then they quit. The children ran into trouble rather quickly, sometimes of a serious nature. We need to follow this instruction to bless our children with the priestly blessing. YHVH honors it and blesses us for it. When we don't, the family will suffer for it. Why is it so important? Your children can see that you care about them enough to pray over them and bless them. You are showing them honor, which in Hebrew means to give them value as a person. You are showing your child that they are valuable enough to take the time each week to bless them, to show them that YHVH has good things planned for them. When the father stops blessing his children, he has ceased to honor them. They think they no longer have value. Is it any wonder that they soon fall into trouble?

The next thing to include on Friday night is a personal blessing for each child. This could be in the form of a verse, or encouragement for the following week. Some parents put their hand on the child as they bless them. Some pull the child right on their lap. Some whisper something special in their child's ear. It could be as simple as, "I know you're worried about your math test this week. I know you will do well." You might also pray for each child. Perhaps you would pray something like, "Help Sarah to treat her little sister nicely this week."

I would also encourage you to include the Children's Ketubah in your Friday night blessings. Perhaps you could read it out loud. Take time privately to review it and evaluate yourself. Pray for help in the coming week. If you are feeling brave, ask your children how you are doing. Their frankness will be your best progress report. Take Shabbat to start anew each week. Maybe last week was rough, but this week is a fresh start. Make the best of it.

Honor thy father and thy mother: that thy days may be long upon the land which the LORD thy God giveth thee.

Exodus 20:12

Our children are commanded to honor us. This does not simply mean to obey. It means to show value. How will they learn to honor and value us as their parent? We demonstrate honor each Shabbat as we pull them on our lap and bless them. We demonstrate it every day when we listen to them and pray for them. We show them value when we teach them skills that they will need. We honor them when we properly and lovingly discipline them. Everything in this ketubah is another way to show honor and value and love to your children. As they grow up being loved and valued, they will learn to treat the people in their life with honor as well.

That is what this book is all about. We need to break the chain of mediocrity in parenting. We need to raise up a generation of children that are loved and know how to love. They need to love and obey their Heavenly Father because they saw us loving and obeying Him. I hope this book can be a tool to that end. I pray that you will join me in this project. Will you step out on a limb and choose to be accountable? Will you sign a ketubah for your children? I know it will change your life and theirs. How do I know that? Because it is changing ours.

Shalom Alecheim! May YHVH bless you and keep you.

Chapter 4

Additional Resources

Study to shew thyself approved unto God, a workman that needeth not to be ashamed, rightly dividing the word of truth.

2 Timothy 2:15

Resources

Anne of Green Gables, DVD, 1986. I quoted from this movie in the book, and feel it is a wonderful movie for young girls. Though Anne is far from perfect, she learns to apologize, let go of grudges, and remain true no matter what.

Betrothed, DVD, Brayden and Talitha Waller. This is the beautiful and real life story of the betrothal and wedding of the Wallers.

Blessed be the Man, by Lynda Coats. This high school curriculum based on Psalm 1 is the boy's equivalent of Far Above Rubies, described below.

Boy Scouts Handbook: The First Edition, 1911. This book covers a wide array of skills necessary for boys and girls. While some information is outdated, it is still a valuable resource.

Far Above Rubies, by Lynda Coats. This high school curriculum is based on Proverbs 31 and covers all the subject areas. Girls will choose various projects to complete, such as reading good books, doing research projects, interviews, and more. I used this some when I was in high school. Very good.

For Instruction in Righteousness, by Pam Forster, Doorposts. This book takes all the major categories of sin, and gives Scripture, Bible stories, natural consequences, and positive character qualities for each. It is indispensable for putting Scripture at the center of your child's upbringing.

Guardian Angel, by Skip Moen. This book gives a clear picture of the ezer kenegdo, the helpmate. He pulls insight directly from the Hebrew.

Homeschooling Torah, by Anne Elliott. This is a complete homeschool curriculum specially designed for Torah observant families.
www.homeschoolingtorah.com

Mama's Torah: The Role of Women, by Batya Wooten. Batya gives a refreshing and Scriptural picture of the spiritual influence of a woman in the home.

Plants Grown Up, by Pam Forster, Doorposts. This book is a very thorough character study for boys. It is designed to be used K-12, and would be ideal for working with more than one son at the same time. Memory verses, research projects, service ideas, writing assignments and more are all included.

Polished Cornerstones , by Pam Forster, Doorposts. This book is a very thorough character study for girls. It is designed to be used K-12, and would be ideal for working with more than one daughter at the same time. Memory verses, research projects, service ideas, writing assignments, and more are all included.

Raising Real Men, by Hal and Melanie Young, 2010. This book was written by the parents of six boys. The authors are very real about what boys are really like. I learned to embrace my boys and envision what they can become.

Take Two Tablets Daily, by Angus Wooten. This book is a list of the 613 commands with Scriptural references.

The Ten Realities, by Dr. Frank Seekins, 2010. This audio teaching will revolutionize the way you think about the ten commandments. Dr. Seekins demonstrates the importance of honor in family life.

Torah Family Living, by Heidi Cooper. This is my website where you will find articles, homeschool materials, and more to help you make Torah the center of your home.
www.torahfamilyliving.com

Hebrew 4 Christians This site has the weekly Shabbat blessings in English and Hebrew. It is designed to be easy to use and learn. There are also materials to help you read and learn the weekly Torah portion.
www.hebrew4christians.com

My First Torah – This is a beginner reader version of the Torah portions, with hand drawn illustrations.

Torah Family Living Writing Series- This series consists of six workbooks to help your child write and learn about Scripture.

Level One- Your young student will trace verses from each Torah portion.

Level Two- Give your child an introduction to Hebrew as they copy Psalm 119 , learn the aleph bet, and 176 Hebrew words.

Level Three- Your child will be copying a passage of Scripture from each Torah portion.

Level Four- Your child will have fun learning about science as they copy verses from Scripture all about YHVH's creation.

Level Five- Your student will practice cursive as they copy Torah.

Level Six- Give your child the opportunity to write original work with writing prompts taken from each Torah portion.

Torah Reading Schedule

The Torah reading schedule starts right after Sukkot each year. You can find many resources and teachings online to help you understand each portion better.

Beresheet	Genesis 1:1-6:8
Noach	Genesis 6:9-11:32
Lech Lecha	Genesis 12:1-17:27
Vayera	Genesis 18:1-2:24
Chayei Sarah	Genesis 23:1-25:18
Toldot	Genesis 25:19-28:9
Vayetzei	Genesis 28:10-32:3
Vayishlach	Genesis 32:4-36:43
Vayeshev	Genesis 37:1-40:23
Miketz	Genesis 41:4-44:17
Vayigash	Genesis 44:18-47:27
Vayechi	Genesis 47:28-50:26
Shemot	Exodus 1:1-6:1
Vaera	Exodus 6:2-9:35
Bo	Exodus 10:1-13:16
Beshalach	Exodus 13:17-17:16
Yitro	Exodus 18:1-20:23
Mishpatim	Exodus 21:1-24:18
Terumah	Exodus 25:1-27:19

Tetzaveh	Exodus 27:20-30:10
Ki Tisa	Exodus 30:11-34:35
Vayakel	Exodus 35:1-38:20
Pekudei	Exodus 38:21-40:38
Vayikra	Leviticus 1:1-5:26
Tzav	Leviticus 6:1-8:36
Shemini	Leviticus 9:1-11:47
Tazria	Leviticus 12:1-13:59
Metzora	Leviticus 14:1-15:33
Acharei Mot	Leviticus 16:1-18:30
Kedoshim	Leviticus 19:1-20:27
Emor	Leviticus 21:1-24:23
Behar	Leviticus 25:1-26:2
Bechukotai	Leviticus 26:3-27:34
Bemidbar	Numbers 1:1-4:20
Naso	Numbers 4:21-7:89
Behaalotcha	Numbers 8:1-12:16
Shelach	Numbers 13:1-15:41
Korach	Numbers 16:1-18:32
Chukat	Numbers 19:1-22:1
Balak	Numbers 22:2-25:9
Pinchas	Numbers 25:10-30:1
Mattot	Numbers 30:2-32:42
Masei	Numbers 33:1-36:13

Devarim	Deuteronomy 1:1-3:22
Vaetchanan	Deuteronomy 3:23-7:11
Eikev	Deuteronomy 7:12-11:25
Re'eh	Deuteronomy 11:26-16:17
Shoftim	Deuteronomy 16:18-21:9
Ki Teitzi	Deuteronomy 21:10-25:19
Ki Tavo	Deuteronomy 26:1-29:8
Nitzavim	Deuteronomy 29:10-30:20
Vayelech	Deuteronomy 31:1-31:30
Ha'azinu	Deuteronomy 32:1-32:52
Vezot Haberakah	Deuteronomy 33:1-34:12

Acknowledgments

First, I want to thank YHVH for creating me and drawing me back to Him. Thank you for giving me creativity and the ability to write. I can't think of a more pleasant way to serve You. Thank you for my seven arrows, and any that we haven't met yet. This book was written to help me be a better mom to them.

I want to thank my husband and best friend. You are always real with me and you love me no matter what. You told me I could do this, and you pushed me when I needed it. I love you!

I must say thank you to my little monkeys, as I affectionately call them. Naomi, Holly, Isaac, Sadie, Elisha, Noah and Caleb – You're all great! You taught me the things I needed to write this book by simply existing. Wait, if you simply existed, my house would always be clean and quiet, and I would be miserable. I love you, noise, mess, and all. Thank you, Noah, for providing the nursing sessions during which this book was written.

Mom and Dad, I love you. Thank you for raising me the way you did. Thank you for homeschooling me. Without your example, I would not be who I am today. Mom, thank you for talking with me on the phone, listening to my ideas, and editing my work. You are as much a friend as you are a mom. Dad, you're one of my greatest cheerleaders, and I will always cherish our walks through the yard.

Thank you to all my readers. By simply reading this book, you have given value to its words. I pray that YHVH blesses you on your parenting journey. If you enjoyed this book, please consider leaving feedback to benefit future readers. Thanks and Shalom!

~ Heidi Cooper

About the Author

I have been married since 2000 to my best friend, Doug. We homeschool our seven children, and live on a farm with a menagerie of critters, from ducks to a donkey. I enjoy providing healthy food for my family, learning about herbs, knitting, and researching school materials for my children. It's a full life, so I am thankful for the time I can spend on my writing.

I am passionate about learning Scripture and especially Torah, which is the foundation for all the rest of Scripture. I enjoy teaching it to my children. I want to see Torah affect people's daily lives. I am amazed at how much YHVH taught me just while writing this book. He has given me so much, and I am happy to have the opportunity to share with others.

I graduated from the Institute for Children's Literature, and am currently pursuing various writing projects such as children's books and homeschool materials. I try to be very real in my writing, only writing the material my own family would use. It is a blessing to see other people benefiting from it as well.

I enjoy writing about our daily life and homeschooling journey on my website: www.torahfamilyliving.com. You can get to know me a little better there. Thank you so much for inviting me into your life for a short time through this book. I hope I was able to be used in a positive way. May YHVH bless you!

Made in the USA
Monee, IL
10 September 2023